D1561654

A MOM'S SHATTERED HEART

Can I Ever Trust God Again?

By Dorothy J. Jones

Dedication

This book is written in memory of my youngest son, Craig, but it is dedicated to God for His Glory, to Jesus His Son and the Holy Spirit for His ever-present comfort.

For God so loved the world, that He gave His only begotten Son, that whosoever believeth in Him should not perish, but have everlasting life. John 3:16 KJV

About the Author

My purpose for writing this book is to tell people about the power of God to transform a life filled with confusion and unhappiness to a life filled with joy, hope, peace and stability, even in the midst of tragedy. The first chapter will give a little background about where God brought me from, so hopefully, you will know that nothing is impossible with God. If He changed me...He can change anybody.

There's a song that says: *'If you could see where Jesus brought me from to where I am today, then you would know the reason why I love Him so'.*

Dorothy J. Jones

Dottie and Tommy

Author's Acknowledgments

Many thanks and God's blessings to Betsy Head, one of my dearest friends. She is the one who encouraged me to step out in faith with this endeavor. She worked patiently with me, gathering information, editing and putting forth countless hours of typing (sometimes into the wee hours of the morning). Best blessings not only to you Betsy, but to Tom and Bobby for their unselfishness of your time.

Thanks to Frances Robinson for her words of encouragement and preparing the book layout, suitable for the publishers' acceptance.

My deepest gratitude and love to my Pastors S. Michael and Marigold Cheshier, my church family, relatives, friends and neighbors who loved, prayed and walked with us hand in hand through the most difficult time of our life.

Thanks to my husband Tommy, who loved me and stuck by my side, through thick and thin.

...A Very Special Thanks to Our Son Brad...

Thank you for your love and unitedness with us in hurting for a season; for your faith and trust in us and in God for believing one day when we view the finished product of this weaving of joy and sorrow in our lives. We will rejoice and be glad. Yes, you will stand with us and say: "*Mama, He did know the end from the beginning. He really did do all things well*".

Thank you, Tommy and Brad, for your enthusiasm and encouragement for me to..."***Go for it!***" I love you both deeper than words can express.

To God be the Glory forever and ever. AMEN.

Table of Contents

WHO IS DOTTIE JONES?

I was raised in a home that partied most every weekend with drinking, arguing and fighting. My dad's mom was a Christian so he was taught moral values that he tried to instill in us. Though he didn't adhere to them, on Sunday mornings when he dropped us off at church, he'd cover up a can of beer in his lap. My parents were very strict but we were well provided for and didn't realize until we were grown how much they loved us and wanted us to do the right things in life.

I met my future husband when I was 14 and just knew he was the one. During our dating years we always went to church on Sunday. He was raised in a Christian home so my family's lifestyle was completely foreign to him. I couldn't wait to graduate so we could get married then I could do what I wanted to do; so, I thought. I wanted to party without any restrictions but he just wanted to settle down.

After being married for a couple of years, we were financially stable and had our own home. We decided it was time to start our family. We tried for the next five years to no avail. After many tests and even trying fertility drugs, I finally got very frustrated and upset. Going to work one morning, I don't know why, but I said: *"God apparently you don't want me to have a baby, so I don't care anymore. I am going to get on with my life".*

Well don't you know, I got pregnant a couple of months later. Brad was born almost seven years after our marriage. We were ecstatic. He was beautiful and healthy. What more could you ask for?   Deep in my heart I knew it was God's doing, even though I didn't know anything about His personal involvement in people's lives.

I guess I had a restless spirit, always wanting to party, like my parents did. Tommy was more of a home body. So needless to say, it didn't take long for problems to arise in our marriage. Through the disappointment of what we both thought our marriage could have been, we began to go down the wrong path. I went into a deep depression and almost total breakdown. We were at the point of divorce.

Because of the love we had for our oldest son Brad, we decided to try to save our marriage, if it were possible. Tommy said let's forget the past and start over. I needed answers so I started going to a psychiatrist to try and find peace with myself. He prescribed medication, but nothing was changing. I only wanted to sleep a lot.

He recommended I go to a psychologist since he couldn't help me. Well, that didn't help either. Nothing he said got rid of my confusion and guilt. He recommended that we go to a marriage counselor together.

After several months of marriage counseling, she suggested that we go back to church because we needed spiritual help to mend our relationship and marriage. (We had been going against the morals of God that our parents had taught us.) Thank God for her wisdom and leading of the Holy Spirit because that was the key. That made sense to me so I decided then and there I was going to try the church thing. So, in the summer of 1975, driving home from her counseling session, at a stop light I cried out: *"God if you really exist and if you really can see and hear me now...**Please help me!** I've made a mess of my life".* I felt goose bumps all over my body. I started to cry and laugh at the same time. A peace came over me like I had never known. Believing that it had to be the Lord hearing and touching me – I hollered out loud: *"God please don't ever leave me...it's you and me now...YOU are what I've been looking for all my life."*

I was born again but didn't know it or even understand what that meant. Thank God we did get back in church but after a while Tommy stopped going. He said he was too busy right now and we were getting ready to build a house. He said when he got caught up, he would go with me again.

I accepted that and began reading my bible and learning what I needed to do, not only as a Christian but to be a godly wife and mother. I asked the Lord if I was truly forgiven of my past sins...could we please have another child? (Note...it took almost seven years to have our first son even though we tried everything including fertility drugs.) When I became pregnant within a couple of months, I knew then that God loved me and had forgiven me for the past.

In January 1976 I walked down the aisle in church to confirm my decision to accept Jesus as my Lord and Savior, and later got water baptized. I was 3 months pregnant and felt that my baby was baptized with me. I began reading my bible and going to church as much as possible. I couldn't get enough of learning about the Lord. I was learning how to handle worry and anger the Lord's way – not Dottie's way.

My life began to drastically change. My mom thought I was going to have a nervous breakdown if I didn't slow down. Needless to say, it also began to cause conflict with my husband. He couldn't believe that I didn't want to do the things I used to do. I was getting on his nerves. I thought he didn't want me to be a Christian. He told me later he just wanted to make sure that I was serious and not getting into some new fad.

I had to learn how to be sensitive to my husband's

feelings and in time he would join me in my new found faith. The Lord began restoring our marriage.

> Therefore, if any man be in Christ, he is a new creature: old things are passed away; behold, all things are become new. II Cor. 5:17 KJV

Tommy, Brad, Craig and Dorothy (Dottie) Jones

GOD'S CHAIN OF ORDER

Shortly after our second son Craig was born, I remember the Lord woke me up one night and asked me if He was first in my life. It shocked me because I didn't know how to answer. Why was He asking me that? I started thinking about it but fell back asleep. The next night the same thing happened and He told me to think about it some more so I did all the next day. The third night He asked me the same thing again and I said: "*Lord you know I can't lie to you because you would know if I did. Tommy is first, Brad is second, Craig is third and you are fourth.*"

In my mind I thought I was giving Him a pretty good ranking since I couldn't see Him or hug Him like I could them. *"You know I love you and I wouldn't give you up for anything but I'm having problems with Tommy over you already. If I put you first, I'm afraid I will really be in trouble with him."*

He told me there was an order in His kingdom and He must be first. Then He said, "*If you will put me first, I will give you even more love for your husband and children. I'm not trying to take from you...I'm trying to give to you."*

With tears in my eyes, I said: *"OKAY God, I'll put you first."* I didn't know how I was going to do it or how my marriage would be affected, but I was determined to try. God would have to help me with this new arrangement.

Looking back, it was the best decision I ever made and thank God I did! I've never removed God from His number one position even with all my grief, anger and pain. He had shown me in order to receive His full strength and help in my life He would have to be in first place. I couldn't have come through Craig's death any other way.

Thou shalt have no other gods before me.
Exodus 20:3 KJV

A NEW LIFE BEGINS FOR US

We moved to Lacombe, Louisiana in 1978, and built our home on Bayou Powell. Life was good. I started going to a bible study and was looking for a church. A friend told me about a church named Northlake Assembly of God in Covington. The Pastor was S. Michael Cheshier and his wife Marigold. She gave me a cassette tape of his preaching and her singing. I knew that was where I wanted to go to church. I also bought her music cassette tape. It was so anointed and uplifting that I played it over and over. Glad I did because I never knew how much one of those songs would encourage and give me hope in the future.

Pastor S. Michael and Marigold Cheshier

My husband drove me to Covington (about 25 miles) to show me the way there so I could go to church the following Sunday. He finally believed I was serious about being a Christian. As I stepped through the double doors that first Sunday morning, I sensed the Lord say: "*This is your home*". I was so happy.

At my new church that first morning I felt as though God was testing my commitment. The pastor was preaching on the sufficiency of God's grace to go through anything. Could we really trust God with our lives no matter what? A battle began raging in my mind. Suddenly I remembered hearing a testimony at a Ladies Aglow Meeting a couple of months before of a couple who lost three of their children in a car wreck. I thought, Oh Lord, I could never go through anything like that. I knew I wasn't mentally or spiritually strong enough.

My mind was racing. Would I still love the Lord if that happened to me? He had taken care of me so far, so nervously I said: "*Yes Lord, I will never turn my back on you no matter what if you will help me and give me your grace."* Little did I know the importance of my response.

When I got home, I told Tommy I finally found the church I had been looking for and that the Pastor announced he needed help in the office. He said, *"Well, you ought to see if he has typing or something you can do at home".*

I attended the Wednesday night service with both boys and told him I could help but would have to bring typing home. He said that would be fine.

I went back Friday to pick up the paperwork but the pastor wasn't there so I called him and said I would get it Sunday morning. As fate would have it, on Saturday February 23, 1980 our lives changed forever. All I can say is thank God I found my church home.

> Trust in the Lord with all thine heart; and lean not unto thine own understanding. In all thy ways acknowledge Him, and He shall direct thy paths. Proverbs 3:5-6 KJV

Brad, Tommy and Craig

TRAGEDY STRIKES

February 20, 1980 was our oldest son Brad's ninth birthday. Because the date fell on a Wednesday, we planned to celebrate his birthday on Saturday, February 23, 1980.

The night before I was busy putting icing on the cake when Craig (our youngest son who was three and half years old) came running into the kitchen. He immediately spotted the bowl of red icing, jumped up on the bar stool, and asked: *"Momma can I have some?"*

Brad added, *"Can we have the bowl when you finish?"*

I started to say no because Craig already had his bath and was ready for bed. However, against my better judgment I said "Yes". My heart melted when I saw the excitement on his precious little face and those big blue eyes. I knew he was going to be a mess after and need another bath. Sure enough he did. He had red icing from head to toe. It tickled me to see him and Brad enjoying that little treat. I thank God to this day that I didn't rob them of that pleasure.

It was back to the bathtub again. This time as I put on his pajamas, his face and blonde hair seemed to shine brighter to me than normal. I figured it was because he was so full of excitement about the party the next day. As he usually did, he wrapped his arms around my neck and said: *"Mama I luuuuve you!"*

I squeezed him tight and said: "*I love you too Tootsie*".

Craig at 3 years old

Craig had a habit of talking himself to sleep every night as he filled his dad in on all the happenings of the day. This night was different. He just lit up as he began to name every relative and person he knew. He started off by saying *"I love Bubby"* (that's what he called his big brother Brad).

One by one he attached the words "**I love**" to each name. I didn't think he would ever stop naming relatives and friends. I don't know what was different, but there was something special about the way he listed all of the people he loved. (I thought, I shouldn't have given him that icing.)

The next morning Brad was eager for the day to get started. Today we would celebrate his 9th birthday. Words can't express how much he wanted a football for his birthday. I loaded the boys in the car and headed to the Lacombe Hardware store to get it. They secretly wrapped it so Brad couldn't tell what it was.

We usually sang while we were riding in the car just to pass time. Craig especially loved Christian music and he always sang along with the tapes I had. He knew those songs by heart. On the way home we tried to agree to sing a song we all knew and liked. Well because the boys couldn't agree on singing the same song, I said: *"Well I'll pick the song. Let's sing Hallelujah...Hallelujah".*

We sang it all the way home. Looking back, I can see how God was preparing us for what was about to transform our lives forever.

We lived on a bayou with a dock and boat slip. Craig wasn't allowed to play outside without me, his dad or his brother with him. Being a Christian, I knew fear was not of God, but I had a fear. Fear of him and the bayou. After all, Craig was only three and a half years old, and definitely not old enough to play outside by himself.

I really wanted to **trust** the Lord to protect and always take care of my boys. Because we had a lot of glass doors and windows across the back of the house, I let Craig play with his trucks and cars on the patio for short periods of time where I could see him while I was cleaning or cooking. I know I must have drove that baby crazy because if I didn't hear or see him for a moment, I would sing: "*Craig where are you?*"

He would put his face on the sliding glass door and sing right back: *"I right here!".*

Little did I know that this would be the clincher of my healing. Could God be trusted or not?

When we arrived home, I fed the boy's lunch. They wanted to go outside and wait for Brad's friend Kevin, to cross the bayou in his flat boat, and the other kids to arrive for the party.

While he waited, Brad rode his mini bike on a path he had made in our yard. That day, as he rode around and around on it, Craig followed him on his tricycle.

Brad on his Mini Bike

Craig on his Trike

I began setting up for the party inside. Brad was so anxious to get his gift (hoping it was a football) that he kept coming in and out the house asking me to let him open it. I kept saying, *"No"* you need to wait for the party to begin, so he went back outside and probably made a few more loops around the yard before coming back in again.

Due to dealing with PMS, I felt out of sorts and decided to lay on the couch for a moment. Just as I laid down, he came back inside to see how much longer he had to wait. I figured I might as well get up and went into the kitchen. With him following me, I took the chicken out of the refrigerator and placed it in the sink to start preparing it for supper. I said, "*Brad, go back outside with your brother and wait until the kids get here*".

As he was heading outside, I looked out all of the windows to see if I could spot Craig on his trike. I started feeling really uneasy when I didn't see him. I ran outside hollering: ***"CRAIG! CRAIG! Where are you?"***

 Brad was calling him too. No answer. Fear gripped me like a vice around my chest. I thought: **OH NO! THE WATER!** I started running to the left of the property toward the bayou and told Brad to go look on the right side. I was in panic mode running, hollering and crying. It scared Brad so much that he started running toward me crying. As I approached the boat slip there was my baby floating on top of the water, face down. I jumped into the water and grabbed him up in my arms. I screamed with all my might... *"GOD!"*

When I leaned him back over my arms his beautiful blue eyes just rolled back. I began shaking him and calling his name hoping he would come to and start breathing. I waded toward the dock to lay him up there but I wasn't tall enough to reach it. Poor little Brad was standing there motioning with his hands and begging me to hand Craig to him. I guess I was in shock because I couldn't bring myself to let go of him. I don't remember how but we both were able to get him on the dock.

I was screaming so loud, that my neighbor Ellis (who lived across the bayou) ran out and jumped in his flat boat to try to get to us, but he couldn't get the motor started.

The nurse who lived down the street heard me and

came running. She immediately started CPR. I put my hands on her back praying and quoting every scripture I could think of. I knew God had the power to revive him and believed He would. I was a desperate mother in a desperate situation. God had, after all, given us this child. Surely, He wouldn't take him away from us.

The paramedics arrived and I asked one of them why they weren't going to put their machine on Craig to make him breathe. (I couldn't even think of what it was called.) He just looked at me and shook his head. He was trying to avoid telling me the truth. Finally, he said that they were unable to put Craig on a resuscitator because they didn't have one with them. I pleaded with them to take Craig to the hospital to put him on one.

Everyone there knew he was gone but me. One of the paramedics told me to go inside and get a blanket. That gave me hope. When I got to his room, Brad was kneeling at the foot of his bed praying for God to let his little brother live. I ran back outside with the blanket and our friend Cliff, grabbed and held me back.

I said, "*Please Cliff, let me go, I have to give them this blanket*".

He said, "*Dottie, I can't let you go over there*".

"*Why? What's going on? He's going to be alright, isn't he?*"

He began to cry and hold me tighter. Something wasn't right. I suddenly realized something was very wrong. I started crying and begged Cliff to at least let me go sit on the dock steps near Craig so I could talk to God and figure out what was going on. Reluctantly he let me go.

As I sat on the bulkhead trying to comprehend what was happening, I thought maybe I prayed wrong by not quoting the right scriptures. Then I thought: that's not it – oh God, it's because you're going to perform a miracle, aren't you? That was it! God was going to show all these people standing here a miracle by raising Craig up. I believed nothing was impossible with God. There was no doubt in my mind about His power; after all, He raised Lazarus from the dead.

I started crying and talking to the Lord again. *"Please talk to me! Please don't take Craig! You're All Mighty God!"* I was grasping at any straw to get my baby back. I thought: *"You've never failed me!"*

All of a sudden it hit me, that's it, that's what God wants me to holler out so everyone there would know He could be trusted and was faithful. Just as I started to scream out as loud as I could: "**GOD YOU HAVE NEVER FAILED ME!**" ...

...Instantly the Lord said: "***Don't do that! Dottie, I have never failed you and I'm not failing you now. Get up and go inside***".

I couldn't believe this was happening. As I walked back to my house, the fact that Craig was dead and God wasn't going to revive him, suddenly began to sink in. I was totally devastated. I couldn't believe I was actually going through this. I thought I would do anything for God but not this.

Friends accompanied me to the house trying to

comfort me. I was in such a daze that Zelda, my friend, had to tell me I needed to change out of my wet clothes.   I was confused, scared and worried. How was I going to tell Tommy what happened? How was he going to react?

As I entered the living room the police were there. I looked at the officer, held out my arms to be handcuffed, and told him that I was ready to go. He said, *"What – go where?"*

I said, *"Aren't you going to take me to jail?"*

He said, *"No, I just need some information from you."*

I wanted to go to jail because I felt I had failed as a mother. When the police left, my friend Zelda, took me to my bedroom to change my wet clothes.

Going back into the living room, I sat down by the fireplace and picked up my Bible. Desperately needing an answer, I looked down on the page that was open and read: "*So if you are suffering according to God's*

will, keep on doing what is right and trust yourself to the God who made you, for He will never fail you.'"
I Peter 4:19 TLB

I knew that the Lord was speaking to me through His Word. He was there and in control. I began to calm down and knew He would bring me through this because He promised to never leave me or forsake me.

One of my friends remembered me talking about my new church so she called it hoping to get in touch with the Pastor. As God would have it, he was on the church roof with other men, doing some repairs. He said he heard sirens and felt like something bad had happened. Someone called him down off the roof to tell him what just happened. He said as he went into his office to clean up, (and for some unknown reason he had a suit hanging in the closet) so he was able to change immediately.

Pastor Cheshier came, and with close friends by my side, we waited for Tommy to come home. (Back then there were no cell phones, so we just had to wait.)

I dreaded the moment when he would walk through the door. I didn't know how he was going to react. I was full of hurt and fear. I thought...God this really did it...there isn't any chance of him wanting to give his heart to you now. As much as he loves that baby it will be impossible.

The dreaded moment arrived. Seeing the cars in front of the house, Tommy said he suspected something bad had happened. Bursting through the door, he questioned, "**What's happened?**"

I could see panic written all over his face.

"Where are my kids?"

Trying to think of how and what to say, I said: *"Please don't make me tell you...**please**!"*

"*Tell me what?*"

"*It's Craig...he drowned.*"

"Where is he?" Tommy asked, *"Is he at the hospital? I want to see him".*

"You can't", Dottie replied.

"Why not?" Tommy asked.

"Because, he's at the funeral home already."

I waited to see him become enraged, but instead, he just stood there in silence. One of our friends went to him and put his arms around him to somehow cushion the shock. Breaking into tears he sat down and just stared into space. Pastor Cheshier went over to Tommy and said: *"Let's go get alone and pray".*

We went to our bedroom, and with Brad between us, knelt beside the bed. Our little family began to cry out for God to help us deal with the anguish and pain in our hearts.

About that time, Pastor's wife, Marigold, came into the room. Together they began ministering to us. Tommy's heart was crushed. He looked at Marigold and asked: *"Why did God take my son?"*

Marigold said with such assurance: *"Tommy I don't know why God chose to take your little son home to be with Him – but one thing I'm sure of - just like when King David's son died because of his sin with Bathsheba, King David said: he can't come back to me but I will go to him."* (2 Samuel 12:23)

That scripture penetrated Tommy's heart and with a made-up mind he said: *"I can promise you one thing - I will see my son again too!"*

There in our bedroom he knelt and gave his heart and life to Jesus Christ. Over the years he has served as a Sunday school teacher, Men's Ministry Officer and Deacon in our church. To this day he has never turned back from serving the Lord.

SUNDAY- MAKING FUNERAL ARRANGEMENTS

The next day Tommy's parents took us to make the funeral arrangements. The thought of that shook me to my core. I thought I would probably faint and fall out. I never thought I would have to go through something like this. Is this really happening or am I dreaming? This can't be real! Is there something I should have done that I didn't? If only I had gone out the door sooner Craig might still be alive. As I leaned my head back on the seat of the car, I sensed the Lord saying: *"My timing is perfect".*

I shared that word with Tommy. He had also been thinking – if only – because he was hurting too. He told me he was remembering all the times Craig would sing: *"He brought me out of the miry clay; He set my feet on a rock to stay".*

He looked at me and said: *"He did put his feet on a rock to stay and He will never fall because he's with the Lord".*

I've heard it said that it is not natural for a child to die before the parents. I guess we're just geared to think that it will never happen to us. It's quite an unbelievable shock when it does.

There were so many decisions to make in such a short time. Where would Craig's resting place be? Thanks to our neighbors for suggesting a cemetery close to our home. To make matters worse we only had $13 in the bank. How would we pay for everything? Thank God for Tommy's parents who helped us financially.

What would we dress Craig in? I remembered I recently cleaned a sport coat for him to wear for Easter. (It had belonged to Brad.) I intended to buy pants to go with the coat but hadn't yet. Now that I needed them, it was Sunday, and stores were closed. My friend, Zelda, knew a lady with a small clothing store, who graciously opened it so she could get the pants. I really appreciated the sensitivity of so many people.

Driving to the funeral home, people were passing by in their cars happy and laughing while I was in our car scared and dreading making the arrangements. Thoughts of Craig never graduating from school – going to college – getting married and having children caused me to start crying because he would never experience those special moments in life. The Lord spoke to my heart and said: "*Those things are not the most important in life – making Heaven is and Craig has achieved the greatest victory*".

The arrangements went better than I ever dreamed they could - only by the grace of God.

And it is He who will supply all your needs...
Phil. 4:19 KJV

PREPARING FOR THE WAKE

Pastor Cheshier came over and suggested we pray before going to the wake. Even after praying I still felt uneasy. Tommy kept looking at me and asked me if I was alright. I said: "*No, I keep hearing the song in my mind...Let us have a little talk with Jesus. That's what I need to do.*"

I went into the kitchen to get something to drink and think about what to do next. I really needed the Lord's peace and assurance to get us through this tragedy. I thought I had it all together so I headed back to the bedroom to wait until it was time to get dressed. As I walked through the living room where family and friends were sitting; I smiled at them to make them think I was okay...but I definitely wasn't. As I entered the bedroom, I felt like I was going to pass out.

Pastor Cheshier said, "*Grab her she's going into shock*".

They laid me on the bed and started praying. I began crying uncontrollably and praying out loud in the spirit.

Tommy had never heard me pray like that before but I didn't care who heard me. I was grieving and felt like I was dying inside.

While I was praying, I had a vision at the same time. I saw the Lord walking down a road carrying His cross. The sight of Him so badly beaten and exhausted broke my heart. As He neared me, He stumbled and fell in front of me, holding Himself up on one knee. I was standing there crying with my hands cupped together holding my grief tight against my chest. He turned His face toward me and looked straight into my eyes with so much love I could hardly stand it.

He said, *"Dottie lay your grief down on my cross".*

I said, *"No Lord, I don't want to put any more weight on you, because your cross is too heavy already".*

He said, **"You <u>HAVE</u> to... you won't be able to carry it... I will carry it for you**. *If you don't, your love for Craig is so strong, that you and Tommy will not make it".*

> Surely, He hath borne our griefs, and carried our sorrows... Isaiah 53:4 KJV

At that moment, I could see by the look on His face, that He was hurting for me. So, with much hesitation, I stooped down to obey Him. As I did, the pain and fear in me left immediately. Overwhelmed with unbelievable excitement of what I had just experienced, I sat up and told those around me what I just saw and heard. That episode with the Lord enabled me to say: "*Y'all it's almost time to go to the wake; I need to take a shower and get dressed".* They looked at me with amazement.

On the way there I began to think that they would never be able to pull me away from the casket; but the Lord assured me that He would help me make it through. I had to know that it was Craig's earthly body in there but that he was alive and well with the Lord. God gave me the strength I needed to be able to see my child in that casket. Never in the world would you have convinced me that I could have done that.

Tommy had been a Christian less than two days, yet God gave him incredible strength, wisdom and grace. As we approached the little casket crying, Tommy lifted his hands towards heaven and said:

"God, you gave him to us and now I totally give him back to you".

Afterward when someone asked how in the world were we able to handle this, we would tell them: *"God had given us Craig, so since He took him back, He must have a special reason for it".*

I felt as though the Lord had put me in a cocoon to enable me to get through the funeral. As friends and loved ones gave their tearful respects to us, all I could think about was that God was going to do something great. My main thought was that the rapture would happen in a couple of days because God knew I couldn't stay separated from my child any longer than that.

When the doors closed that night, we were able to walk out leaving our little boy behind with complete trust in our Lord and supernatural peace in our hearts. I can guarantee you without the Lord I would have gone crazy, lost control, fallen completely apart and need to be heavily sedated. Only by the grace of God I didn't end up an alcoholic, a drug addict or in a mental institution.

THE FUNERAL

The funeral was the next day on Monday, February 25, 1980. Pastor Cheshier did the service. I watched Tommy throughout the funeral hoping and praying that he would not lose the strength God had given him so far. I wanted God to give him the same peace that I was experiencing and God did.

Marigold sang two songs that meant a great deal to me. The first was: "Blessed Assurance" the same song that I played the night of Craig's death. The words were as if Craig was saying to me: *"Momma don't cry...I'm OK...I'm with Jesus and I'm happy and blessed".* The other was "Whatever it Takes" (to draw closer to you Lord, that's what I'm willing to do).

Through the next several days I watched Tommy being blessed as the Lord kept pouring His love on us through those who were in our church, home bible study and friends. Food was constantly brought to our home. Day by day we received cards of encouragement, prayers and money not just from people we knew but from people we didn't know.

We were amazed to see God meet our spiritual and financial needs through others. We felt the Lord's love through these people. At times Tommy's face streamed with tears, tears of a broken heart...broken...but made new by God. We have the hope given to us in God's Word that some glad day we will see Craig and never be separated from him or our loved ones again.

But I would not have you to be ignorant, brethren, concerning them which are asleep, that ye sorrow not, even as others which have no hope.

For if we believe that Jesus died and rose again, even so them also which sleep in Jesus will God bring with him.

For this we say unto you by the word of the Lord, that we which are alive and remain unto the coming of the Lord shall not prevent them which are asleep.

For the Lord himself shall descend from heaven with a shout, with the voice of the archangel, and with the trump of God: and the dead in Christ shall rise first: Then we which are alive and remain shall be caught up together with them in the clouds, to meet the Lord in the air: and so shall we ever be with the Lord.

Wherefore comfort one another with these words.

I Thessalonians 4:13-18 KJV

THE CARPET

A week after the funeral we knew we needed to try and get back to the normal routine of life. That Monday morning my husband had to go to work and Brad had to go back in school. I busied myself preparing lunch kits for them as I had done so many times before. I thought as soon as they're gone, I'll just resume my routine as usual and everything will be just fine. The only problem with that particular logic was that my daily routine and our life had suddenly been interrupted and forever changed just eight days before.

Mondays usually marked the challenge of starting a new week but these past two Mondays were like none that I had ever experienced before. Yes, this Monday morning was different alright. I must confess I started it with much grief and a great deal of fear. Grief of not being able to ever again include Craig in our daily plans or activities. Fear that I would let the Lord down and bring Him much shame because this was one test, I knew I couldn't pass. I knew I didn't have what it took to overcome this tragedy. I couldn't comprehend how

God was going to be able to soothe that unbearable hurt inside of me.

As my husband gave me one last hug before leaving for work his eyes began to search my face. He asked, *"Do you think you'll be alright today being home by yourself?"*

Waves of nausea hit me in the pit of my stomach...by myself! That feeling that had been silently brewing inside of me all morning suddenly broke loose and I fell to my knees crying uncontrollably.

"Oh God please help me! Please help me!" I said, *"Tommy, I can't make it...I feel like I'm dying inside."*

I cried out: *"God please tell me how much longer?"* (Before I see Craig again).

I pleaded with God to tell me. My mind began to race, two weeks, a month, a year, 10 years. "Oh God, it might even be 30 or 40 years! No, God! Please No!"

At that moment, I literally felt like my mind was going to snap because the future frightened me so. I wanted to die so the pain would stop. Our family would never be the same again. How could it be?

Suddenly, the Lord began to calm me down by telling me to look at the carpet across the den and He asked: *"That's a lot of carpet, isn't it?"*

"Yes, Lord", I said.

"Look closer at all the loops in the carpet. Do you think you could count every loop?"

"I don't know...maybe if I could figure out a system," I answered.

"Can you see the strands in each loop?"

"Yes", I said.

"Look even closer", He said. *"Can you see the threads in every strand?"*

"Yes," I said.

"Now do you think you could count every loop, every strand and every thread in that carpet?"

Stunned by these questions, I admitted that this task was too great for me. Even if I figured out a system to begin counting, the number would be too innumerable for me.

Then He said, *"Even if you could count every loop, strand and thread, that number would not even mark the beginning of time in eternity. Now that I've shown you this, look back across that vast area of carpet again. In eternity with me, you will never again experience the pain or separation of death. Understanding this comparison of time, if you were to live another 30 or 40 years without Craig, would I be asking too much of you?"*

Needless to say, when I compared my life span to eternity, I was completely satisfied with His answer. I made it through that day thanking the Lord for the comfort and peace that only He can give.

There were many times since that day that my arms actually ached to hold my son. My heart longed to see his face, even if only at a distance. When I wondered how much longer God, He would reassure me: "*Not much longer...remember the carpet...this life is but a vapor.*"

Anytime I cried out in desperation the Lord always sent just the right Word to help me get through another day. Times such as those deepened my love and trust in Him until this day.

> ...For what is your life? It is even a vapor that appears for a little time and then vanishes away. James 4:14 KJV

BAG OF CLOTHES

Sometime later my sister-in-law, Joyce, came to help and comfort us as we were trying to adjust. She began by going into Craig's bedroom to clear it out of his clothes and things so I wouldn't have to do it. She took his clothes out the chest of drawers and put them in some paper bags. I could see the hurt in her face as she asked me what did I want to do with his clothes. Glancing down at one of the bags, I noticed his new underwear laying on top. I had just bought him '*big boy underwear*' like his bubby.

The reality of his permanent absence hit me again. I started to cry and thought: *"Is this all that is left of him...a lousy paper bag of clothes".*

Immediately it was as if the Lord said: Why are you crying over those rags? I truly believe I heard Him say he's dressed in pure fine linen (trimmed in gold) but I can't confirm that description in the bible.

Those words stunned me; they so blessed and comforted me to be able to let go of that bag of clothes. I told Joyce to put them in the garage and I would give them away later.

I know she had to wonder why one moment I was so upset and the next moment thanking God for such beautiful Words of comfort. All I know is that once again when grief was over bearing, the Lord stepped in to teach me another lesson about His love and mercy.

WHAT NOW?

In the days that followed I would soon discover that it wouldn't be quite so easy for me to surrender as easily as Tommy did. I had the peace and strength to witness to people at the funeral about how loving and great God was; but when it was over...I lost my peace and strength... and I wanted my baby back! I felt like I was on a roller coaster having peace one day and grief the next. I began to comfort myself by assuming that the rapture of the church was going to take place at any moment. As another day would pass, I began to get very uptight. I tried to hope maybe tomorrow would be the day...hang in there Dottie...but the tomorrows kept coming.

There was a battle going on inside of me. I rationalized that since Tommy was born again the day Craig drowned, and I had witnessed to all the people that were put in my life, I figured mission complete...right? I didn't see any reason now for our family to be separated any longer. On the other hand, Tommy handled it much better than me. He was born again the day Craig drowned.

Following the funeral, he began reading his Bible, hours at a time. Tears would flow down his face as the Lord would reveal little nuggets of truth and encouragement to him. He also was giving him the love, wisdom and strength to under gird me during my tormenting battles of guilt, shame, irresponsibility and negligence. Thank God Tommy never blamed me because it would have destroyed me and our marriage.

Only one thing kept me from losing my mind and that was the Word of God. A couple of months later, at an Women's Aglow meeting, I asked for prayer. I was crying and needed an answer as to how in the world did I let this happen to my baby? A lady came up by me and as she was praying for me, she said: "*Jesus is the one who holds the keys to death*". It stunned me because I didn't know who she was.

I really started heaving then because it was as if the Lord said strongly that He held the keys to Craig's death...not Dottie. I had to believe that word and constantly stand on it but it would still take a couple of years for my grief to be healed.

> I am he that liveth, and was dead; and, behold, I am alive for evermore, Amen; and have the keys of hell and of death. Revelation 1:18 KJV

I WILL NEVER LEAVE YOU

One afternoon as I was looking out the windows from my kitchen, I could see all the backyard and the spot in the bayou where Craig had drowned. I couldn't accept the fact that I wasn't with him when he fell in the water. I believed I would have accepted it better had I been near him, because I would have done everything, I knew to do to save him. I couldn't shake the fact that he was all alone. Suddenly these gentle words came to my mind: *"He wasn't alone. He was in my presence before he ever hit the water".*

"What?" I couldn't believe I just heard those words. There are no words to tell you how much comfort and peace came over me at once. I now had the assurance that he wasn't alone. The Lord was with him.

For a long time, I hesitated sharing that thinking someone might not believe it lined up with scripture. The bible says, 'I will never leave you or forsake you.' He is constantly with us in life and death. We do not go through death alone. Craig's body drowned but his spirit was in the presence the Lord. I believe Craig never felt fear because the Lord was with him every moment. When the Lord's Word says...I will never leave you (Hebrews 13:5 KJV), that is exactly what He means...He cannot lie.

Though I walk through the valley of the shadow of death, I will fear no evil for thou art with me.
Psalm 23:4 KJV

THE FIRST MOTHER'S DAY

I looked forward to Mother's Day with dread. Even though that day took on a new meaning since I gave my life to the Lord, today was bringing pain, not joy. I knew that children were blessings from the Lord but one of my little blessings was gone. I wanted both of my boys with me today.

Today should have been a day of thanksgiving for the precious boys God had given me, but I wasn't thankful; I was hurting. Unanswered questions plagued my mind. I desperately needed answers. Sitting in church that day was a battle for me. I didn't want to go to begin with.

The sermon that day was on Proverbs 31, 'The Woman of Noble Character', though I heard very little of it. Turning to Proverbs my mind drifted to those crazy tormenting questions that kept bothering me.

Did Craig wonder why I didn't come and rescue him? What was he doing in heaven now? Did he miss his family? I felt that desperate need to still mother him. After all, I knew what made him happy and what upset him. If he got sad who would comfort and hold him until he fell into a peaceful sleep?

As those crazy questions kept rolling around my head; I glanced down at my bible that was open. Proverbs 8:30 seemed to leap out at me: 'Then I was by Him, as one brought up with Him, and I was daily His delight, rejoicing always before Him.'

As I read that scripture again, it was as if the Lord was giving me the answers. How I needed that Word from the Lord. I was thankful now...knowing Craig was still singing his little songs in the presence of the Lord.

After that, I tuned in enough on the pastor's sermon to hear what he said about mothers raising their children in the fear and admonition of the Lord. I felt a sense of accomplishment because I truly had done that to the best of my ability. Talking about Jesus and singing songs about Him was all he cared about. When he prayed over our meals, he would always turn his face up toward heaven. I know the Lord was looking down at him and smiling. He was what you would call a "FANATIC" (like his mama). Praise the Lord!!!

God poured out His love and grace on me that day and soothed my aching heart. However, suddenly I realized that my other son was hurting too. He was grieving over the loss of his little brother. It wasn't just my loss but it was Brad and Tommy's loss too.

Brad needed his mother and he needed all of her. We had to be sensitive to his grief and reassure him that the joys of life weren't over for him. We had to let him know that we were proud that he was our son, our oldest son, and now our only son. Now would be a time to show him that his dad and I really trusted God. He needed to see our trust in action. Would we follow God in good times as well as the bad times? We had to reinforce to him our love and utmost trust in God's will for our family. Most of all Brad had to know that I was thankful that I was still a mother...**his mother.**

I prayed: Lord please don't let me hurt my son any

more than he already is by being depressed on holidays and special occasions. Don't ever let us feel guilty for being joyful during these times because we should feel joyful if we believe all things work together for good to them who love you.

Please help me to let Brad know how grateful I am that you gave him to us; because he also was a God given miracle. Let him be assured in his heart that someday soon, we will be reunited with Craig and all our loved ones that have gone to heaven, because your Word promises us that. Thank you, Lord, for fulfilling me on this Mother's Day.

> After you have suffered a little while, our God, who is full of kindness through Christ, will give you His eternal glory. He personally will come and pick you up, and set you firmly in place, and make you stronger than ever.
> I Peter 5:10 TLB

ACHING ARMS

There was a time I wanted to hold Craig so bad that my arms actually ached for several days. I thought, *"Oh God, what I wouldn't give to hold him just one more time".*

God answered that request. I had a dream and saw Craig playing in the yard with several children. An older child holding Craig by the hands was swinging him around and around. Losing his grip, he accidentally dropped him. Starting to cry, and with outstretched arms, Craig came running towards me for comfort. Needless to say, I ran toward him just as fast. As I leaned over to pick him up, he wrapped his legs around my waist and his arms securely around my neck. Crying pitifully, he snuggled his head under my chin. I held him as tight as I could, kissing, patting and reassuring him that he was alright.

I don't know how long our time together lasted, but when I woke my arms no longer ached. As I had comforted my child, so had my Father comforted me.

Dottie, Craig and Peanut

Delight thyself also in the LORD: and He shall give thee the desires of thine heart. Psalm 37:4 KJV

FIRST CHRISTMAS

Our first Christmas without Craig was rough. When I went Christmas shopping, I tried to avoid aisles with toys we had bought for him the year before. Christmas morning came and there was an empty place under the tree; there were no presents for Craig.

We could tell that Brad felt a little awkward and nervous. We sat down in front of the tree just looking at one another searching for the right place to start. Tommy said, *"I think we need to pray before we open any gifts"*.

We each thanked God for a beautiful Christmas day. We told the Lord we were hurting and were missing Craig. We asked him to please help us get through that day. Brad specifically asked the Lord to wish Craig a Merry Christmas!

As our healing progressed to the next Christmas, the pain of his absence was not quite as bad. Thank God, as time went on, the holidays brought sweet and precious memories instead of pain.

> In everything give thanks: for this is the will of God in
> Christ Jesus concerning you. I Thess. 5:18 KJV

Brad, Dottie and Tommy
1981 - One year after losing Craig

MOTHER'S DAY AGAIN

May 1981, another Mother's Day without my baby boy. The ache in my heart started up again. I was missing him a lot. Oh, how I wished to God that I could just see his face once more, to satisfy that longing in my heart, even if he was a block away.

I was singing in the choir that morning. We were singing a chorus that says, 'He's worthy, Jesus is worthy, worthy the lamb that was slain'. I knew in my heart that Jesus was worthy of praise no matter what the circumstances, but I couldn't sing those words. I was hurting and wanted my son back, I wanted to hold him, talk to him and hear his little voice again.

Then the choir began to sing 'Bless the Lord O My Soul and all that is within me bless His holy name.' I thought I can't continue to stand here in the choir with my mouth shut and tears streaming down my face. I felt like everyone could see the hurt and anger in my face. I was hurting so much I wanted to run out of the church but knew that wasn't the right thing to do. I silently prayed: Lord, please help me. I knew from past experience that when I began to praise God my grief would leave. Suddenly the thought came to command my soul to sing. I said, *"Soul, you will bless the Lord whether you want to or not".*

I began to weep and sing "Bless the Lord, O My Soul" and all of a sudden, I saw a vision of Craig. He was laying on his stomach with his chin propped up on his fists. The look on his face was one of purest joy and contentment letting me know God is worthy no matter what. With that, the vision faded and my heart broke in repentance to God, for my anger towards Him.

God hadn't forgotten me and He knew what I needed to ease the hurt I had. When was I going to learn that God would never ever fail me? I began to thank Him immediately for letting me see my son's face, if only for a brief moment, it was just what I needed.

Once again, His mercy met my need and my desire. He had given me a special gift this Mother's Day that only He could give. Much of the Psalms contain songs and praises unto God. I learned a great lesson that day...He wants us to step out in faith and truly praise Him, not because we feel like it at the moment, but because He is truly worthy...HE IS GOD.

That was the last Mother's Day that I would grieve like that. One year later I would be totally healed from the grief of Craig's death.

Bless the Lord, O my soul: and all that is within me, bless His holy name. Bless the Lord...
Psalm 103:1 KJV

WHY LORD – WHY?

A couple of months after the funeral, Pastor Cheshier and Tommy kept encouraging me to begin working at the church as secretary. I didn't want to. I didn't feel like I was ready yet and I didn't want to be around people. I just wanted to be by myself to cry when I wanted to. After several months I gave in. I figured since I had to take Brad to school and pick him up in Covington I may as well. Maybe working there might help with my grief and loneliness during the day.

Several ladies came into my office every morning before going into the sanctuary to pray. When finished, they came back in again, full of joy and praising the Lord for such a great time of prayer. As I listened to their excitement, I would think if they had gone through what I had, they wouldn't be so happy. (Woe is me again!)

I had lost my joy. I was grieving, angry and miserable. To top it off, news on the television seemed to constantly report news about children miraculously saved by CPR that had been under water way longer than Craig. I read about choking victims being revived and Boy Scouts who saved and revived drowning victims. When I heard the news or read magazine articles, I became infuriated that I didn't remember those life saving techniques that I learned as a Girl Scout. Why was I being bombarded with hearing this news now? What in the world was going on with me? I dealt with these and other tormenting questions and thoughts a lot before I was healed.

After boohooing and fussing with the Lord all day about why He allowed Craig to drown, I finally said: *"I am so upset with you I don't want to talk to you anymore right now".*

He said, *"OK, I'll be waiting for you whenever you're ready to talk again".*

For me to be as mad as I was, He answered me with the gentlest Words I had ever heard. His loving response broke that anger in me again. What a loving God He is.

I never felt condemned by the Lord for crying or

expressing to Him what I was thinking or feeling. That's all I knew to do.

When I came to a place where I had a hard time coping, I would pray and just be honest with Him. His Word gives us that privilege. At those times, without fail, it was like the Lord sent someone to speak a Word of encouragement to me.

Many times, when I'd read my bible, just the perfect scripture stood out to give me hope. I often read books about others who had gone through such heartache too. Their stories strengthened me and I hoped one day mine would help someone else too.

Blessed be God, even the Father of our Lord Jesus Christ, the Father of mercies, and the God of all comfort; Who comforteth us in all our tribulation, that we may be able to comfort them which are in any trouble, by the comfort wherewith we ourselves are comforted of God. II Cor. 1:3-4 KJV

BEGINNING OF ACCEPTANCE

As the months began to pass, I accepted Craig's death but still wasn't happy about it. Going to work one morning, I told the Lord that I still loved Him, and would serve Him, but I knew my attitude wasn't bringing Him any glory. Life had become very serious to me. I had one goal in mind and that was to get to heaven. Things that others thought was funny...I didn't. I didn't laugh anymore. I had no joy.

How could I possibly be joyful over the death of my child. I couldn't comprehend ever being happy again. I was existing...going through the motions of life one day at a time...just existing. As I drove up to the church, I sat in the car with my head on the steering wheel and cried out to the Lord: *"You know you broke my heart. If I am ever going to be of any benefit to you Lord, my joy has to be restored – you've got to heal this pain and grief. I don't know how you will do it, but I am willing to let you".*

I felt the Lord say: *"Your heart wasn't just broken...*

*...it was **shattered**".*

Instantly I saw a vision of my shattered heart.

Then I saw the <u>pieces</u> being sealed back together one piece at a time. I realized He was showing me that every hurdle I won victory over, He had sealed up, but one piece remained unsealed. I could sense He wasn't disappointed with me. I knew He would complete my healing when I was ready...but it <u>would</u> take time.

> He heals the brokenhearted, binding up their wounds. Psalm 147:3 TLB

THE TRICYCLE AND MY HEALING

Sometime after the accident, Tommy asked me if Craig fell into the water with his trike. (He thought Craig had gone into the water with it.) I said he hadn't so he wanted to know where was the tricycle. On the day of his drowning, he was riding his tricycle while Brad rode his mini-bike. I wasn't aware that it was missing or what had happened to it.

The next day, Zelda told me that she took it to her house until we decided if we wanted to keep it, or give it away. She didn't want us to have it as a grievous reminder. When she told me that, I completely trusted her with his tricycle, and knew it would be there when I wanted it back. She was a great neighbor and friend. (Her son Kevin and Brad were friends.) I thought that maybe someday I would give it to Brad's first child or some needy child.

During the next two years I didn't think much about it because I knew it was safe until I wanted it. Finally I reached a point where I thought I was healed enough to get his tricycle. I planned to put it up in the attic until we decided what to do with it.

One afternoon, on the way home from picking Brad up from school, I stopped at the supermarket to get a few things for dinner. I had the tricycle so strongly on my mind that I decided this was the day to get it. I just knew I was ready. As I stood in the checkout line, I noticed Zelda behind me. I thought that was my confirmation from the Lord. I said, *"Hey Z, it's so good to see you. I feel like the Lord has healed me to the point that I'm ready now to get Craig's trike back from you."*

To my surprise her whole countenance fell as if in shock. She said, *"Oh my God! Dottie, I don't have it; it's gone!"*

I said, *"Gone! What do you mean...Gone?"*

"I was hoping you would never ask me for that trike", Zelda said. *"When we took it, we put it in our shed. When Kevin went out there to play, he became so upset*

at seeing it, we moved it into our attic. When he went into the attic to get old toys and saw it, it still upset him. We didn't want to upset you by bringing it back so we gave it to a needy child. Dottie, we honestly thought you had forgotten about it since it has been so long. I don't know if they have it, but if they do, I will get it back for you."

Sensing the hurt Zelda was feeling, I tried in my disappointment to assure her, that it was okay and not to worry about it.

What she said caused my heart to sink. I couldn't believe what she had done. I could see from the look on her face that she was so sorry and hurt over the anguish she saw in my face. She had, from a loving heart, done the thing that she thought best for my sake. As it turned out, it was best, because God would use that incident to complete my healing.

I reassured her, "This must be what God wanted done with the trike. Please don't be upset, I promise I will be okay".

I could tell that my assurances to her were falling on deaf ears. I think we both left the store in a complete daze.

Craig's Trike

Driving home my mind began reeling trying to grasp what had just happened. I wanted to get angry with Zelda for giving the trike away; but I couldn't. I said,

"God you knew that trike was at her house and you could have kept it there for me, but you didn't. Why did you let that happen? Why?"

It reminded me of the day I trusted God with Craig and when I went to get him, he wasn't there either. For two years I had been learning to trust God all over again, and now that was being destroyed. It felt like I was reliving the day of his death all over again.

Arriving home, I called my pastor, and asked him to pray for me. He offered to come over, but I refused, knowing that this was to be somewhat of a show down between me and God.

I told Brad that I needed to go to my room for a while to talk to the Lord. As I closed the door, the same pain I felt the day I saw Craig floating in the water, hit me like a ton of bricks. I fell to my knees and tears of grief began to pour out of my soul as if a dam had burst. After squalling for some time, I began to spout out my hurt and anger to God:

"I don't understand what you're doing. I trusted you to take care of Craig and I trusted you to take care of the tricycle...now they're both gone. Even though your word says you would never fail me; I feel like you have. You were always so good to me. How can you love me and yet hurt me so bad? I feel like I am dying. I still loved and trusted you even though I didn't understand why you gave Craig to us just to take him back. I believed and told everyone that you had a very good reason and purpose for allowing Craig's death. You know what kept me going for these past two years was the hope of being reunited with him again. Now I'm wondering if I will ever see him again. Will we even know each other? Will I be able to hold and kiss him like I used to or will it be like trying to hug a cold hard statue? What do you want from me?"

I was spewing out everything that was in my mind and heart. I didn't hold anything back. I was totally exhausted from crying, and completely broken by God. Moments of silence passed, and then the Lord said to me: *"Let me ask you some questions now. Do you really believe no matter the outcome of any situation, that I am in complete control and do all things for your good whether you understand or not? If you're going to be of any benefit to me now, and abide with me forever, you will have to totally trust me with this situation. I have been teaching you all along to trust me and I have allowed this incident with the tricycle to bring about your complete healing. Furthermore, what if you never see or know Craig again, how will that affect your relationship with me?"*

That was the one thought I dreaded; and the one thing I was petrified to even think about. My mind didn't even want to go there!

Believing I would see Craig again in heaven was what had kept me going through my grief. It was my hope. As I reflected on that question, I had heard it said that if you really loved someone, you would suffer anything for them. My heart's desire (as a mama) was for him to be happy, completely fulfilled, and well taken care of. I was willing to let go of my thoughts and plans if I really believed God's plan for eternity was the best and perfect way.

The battle had now come to a head and I had a very serious heart wrenching decision to make. Fear and confusion hit me like a ton of bricks. I started crying and pleaded with God; *"Please tell me what you want".*

The words came: ***"Tonight you will choose to trust me or not. The decision will be yours".***

Suddenly the Word of God came to my mind...'Eye has not seen, nor ear heard, neither has it entered into the heart of man, the things which God has prepared for them that love Him'.

Immediately, I felt His assurance so strong, that I would be more blessed and satisfied than my mind could ever imagine. Finally, I said, ***"Okay God, please help me. I choose to trust you".***

Slowly as I got up off my knees, I knew the battle was over. A heavy weight was lifted off me and a peace came over me like I hadn't felt since the day I was born again. I had been put through a test that I never dreamed I would have to face. Looking back, to what seemed like such a hard decision to make, I realized was done only by His precious Word. It was the hope and encouragement I needed to remain faithful.

When Tommy came in from work, I tried to tell him what just happened but couldn't find the right words. There was no hurt or pain. I was puzzled. I could tell he didn't comprehend what I had just went through so I finished preparing supper and let it go.

The next morning, I felt an unusual excitement about going to the office. My friends (the church prayer warriors) came into my office to visit like most mornings before going into the sanctuary to pray. Those ladies prayed and walked with me through the grieving process for two years. They knew the roller coaster of peace and anguish that I had been going through. Now I couldn't wait to tell them what had happened the night before.

I began by telling them that last night I had a confrontation with the Lord. He allowed something to happen that caused me to experience the same pain, if not worse, of Craig's death all over again. As I began telling them about it, I could tell they weren't grasping or understanding, what I had gone through. For some reason the impact of the pain was gone. I couldn't explain or feel it.

I couldn't figure out what was happening to me. I started to laugh and cry at the same time. I hollered out loud: "*I believe God has healed me! That's why I can't feel the pain".*

I never dreamed it would happen like this or so quick. What a time we had that morning shouting and praising the Lord for His miraculous work in me.

Throughout that day I was concerned about how Brad was feeling about the loss of the trike. No doubt he heard me crying and saw how upset I was the evening before. As we talked about it on the way home from school that evening, I shared with him that I had felt anger and mistrust of God, for letting Craig's tricycle be given away. Now I needed to assure him that if God had allowed me to hurt that bad again, He had a very good reason...and He did! That painful episode brought about my healing and I thanked God the battle was over. He healed me and we don't need to worry about Craig's tricycle anymore.

I have no idea where it is, I explained, but God does. Where ever it is...that's where God wants it to be. If He wants us to have it, He will give it back. If He doesn't, just know it is best and we will accept it.

I wanted Brad to know there are times in our life that there will be pain and things we don't understand but God will work it out for our good.   He wants our total and complete trust.

Soon after arriving home, the doorbell rang and Brad went to answer it. All of a sudden, I heard him scream as he came running to me: *"Momma, Momma come look what God did. You were right; He did know where that tricycle was. Momma we trusted God with it and He gave it back to us!"*

There at the front door stood a little red tricycle. I was

totally shocked to say the least. I couldn't comprehend how it got there. I immediately called Zelda to tell her what had just happened. She told me that she had picked Craig's trike up and gave that child a new one. I thanked her for doing that, and told her not to ever worry or feel bad about giving it away, because God used that situation to bring about my healing.

I don't know if she understood, or really believed me or not, but I wanted her to know that I truly loved her and that she will always be one of my dearest friends. I thanked her again for her love and for sticking by us through our ordeal.

It was out of a compassionate and loving heart that God gave back to us that little insignificant tricycle. He proved to me that He knew where the trike was all the time and it was kept there until the right time to be used in my healing. Needless to say, we were thrilled and very thankful.

We still have the tricycle and are saving it for the time God would have us give it away. Nevertheless, each time I look at that tricycle, it serves as a reminder of the night God totally healed me.

> But as it is written, Eye hath not seen, nor ear heard, neither have entered into the heart of man, the things which God hath prepared for them that love Him.
> I Cor. 2:9 KJV

GOD'S VIEW OF DEATH

Before Craig's death, we lived in Kenner, Louisiana located south of Lake Pontchartrain. It was while we were living there that Brad questioned me about death. Driving him to school each day we passed by several cemeteries. One morning, he asked me: *"Momma why do people die and what happens after they die?"*

Thank God I had read I Corinthians 15:36 -38 the night before. I used a rose as an example. I explained that a rose seed is tiny, ugly and dried up but when we plant it in the ground it comes to life again and becomes a beautiful rose. There is no comparison of a rose seed to the beauty of a rose flower. We don't have to worry about death because the second our body dies our spirit immediately goes to heaven (if we are a Christian). So, when our body is put in the ground, God will resurrect it one day with a beautiful supernatural one.

We will never die again, never be sick, and never be injured again to need stitches. (He liked that promise because he recently had nearly 30 stitches put in his arm after falling off his bicycle onto a boat trailer license plate.)

I also told him that we look upon death as a tragedy, but God looks at it differently. Just like we stand excited at the nursery window waiting to see a newborn baby coming into our family, so He sees our death as our birth into His heavenly family.

Precious in the sight of the Lord is the death of His saints. Psalm 116:15

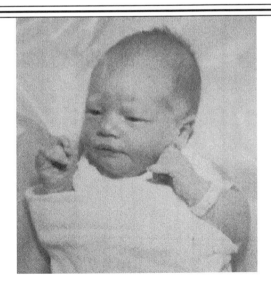

Craig as a Newborn

DEATH IS NOT THE END

When I became a born again Christian, my life was beautiful, and a joy to be alive. I loved the Lord and trusted Him as much as I knew how. But with Craig's death that bubble had burst. I was in a tough situation with my Christian witness. These past few years I had been telling friends and family how wonderful and loving God was. Now what will they think. I wondered how He could stand to see a little boy that He loved drown. How could He stand to see children as well as adults die horrific deaths? How in the world did He even stand to see His only son die? How could a loving and merciful God allow such things? As I thought about that, I believe He gave me a little insight as to how He viewed death.

We think a great deal about our physical bodies and how we are miraculously made. We go to great lengths to take care of it and protect it from as much harm as possible; and we should because it is the temple of the Holy Spirit. But this earthly body is a temporary one. It is natural for us to get so upset and repulsed at the way some deaths occur, but thank God we have His promise...it will be replaced with a new glorious and incorruptible one for eternity.

On the other hand, our soul and spirit will be permanent forever and ever. If we die without accepting the Lord Jesus Christ as our savior, our soul and spirit will be lost forever.   So, the death of the soul and spirit is what repulses Him...because it will never be replaced.   Physical death is temporary; spiritual death is permanent. Death is not the end. It is only the beginning.

For we know that when this tent we live in now is taken down—when we die and leave these bodies—we will have wonderful new bodies in heaven, homes that will be ours forevermore, made for us by God himself and not by human hands. II Cor. 5:1 TLB

And God shall wipe away all tears from their eyes; and there shall be no more death, neither sorrow, nor crying, neither shall there be any more pain: for the former things are passed away. Rev. 21:4 KJV

MAMA DOG

One morning as I looked out of my patio doors, I began to think about relationships on earth, compared to relationships in heaven. I realize family life won't be like it is now. We marry, have babies, raise them to adult hood. Hopefully we'll love each other until death do us part and even beyond the grave.

Naturally because I was missing Craig, I began to wonder if he would remember me being his mama. It's just not normal for a mama to forget her child.

As I looked down at our dog, in my mind's eye I saw a mama dog in a box nursing her puppies. I knew she would take care of them for about six weeks and then start trying to walk away from them so they couldn't nurse anymore. They are usually given away and even if they stayed around her, she wouldn't realize they were once her babies. They would just be other dogs. She goes on with her life like she never knew them. She would never know the experience of loving her babies all of their life.

I thought...thank God humans are not like that...they never forget their young. I felt so sorry for her that she didn't know about the higher sophisticated life we humans have. She wouldn't understand even if I tried to tell her.

As I looked down at that mama dog with pity; I sensed God was looking down at me with pity. Even though God's Word tells us that we don't know how much greater our lives will be in heaven...just like mama dog...I can't comprehend it either.

Can a mother forget her little child and not have love for her own son? Yet even if that should be, I will not forget you. Isaiah 49:15 TLB

THE MINISTER

One day as I was listening to a Christian television station, a minister was teaching that the reason people's prayers weren't answered was because they were not taught the prayer of faith. They weren't praying long enough and not saying the right words.

He told about a woman whose first son had died. When her second son suddenly dropped dead, she became angry, this time at the devil. She said, "*Devil you got one son but you're not getting this one. I'm not going to quit praying until you 'loose' him from death".*

With a laugh the minister said the woman finally caught on to the key. It was the authority and persistence in prayer that brought her second son back to life. I had an overwhelming urge to go kick the TV. As I started toward it the Lord said: *"Stop! I've already spoken to you".*

I asked Him why He allowed this man to say such things and laugh about it. That really upset me. I wondered why I wasn't taught that special prayer. If I had known what he was teaching would Craig be alive today?

Again, guilt hit me...did I not say the right words...did I not quote the right scriptures...did I not have enough faith...did I not pray long enough...did I have an unrepentant sin...did I really believe God's Word...did God really love me? On and on the tormenting questions drove me to my knees. I cried and begged God to help me understand why my prayer for Craig was not answered. I blamed myself for Craig's death and his sermon poured more guilt on me. It just about finished me off.

Gently, I heard the Lord say: *"Dottie, if you would have walked outside and seen Craig drowning, what would you have done?"*

"Lord, I would have run as fast as I could to get him out."

"Would he have had to say just the right words or beg

you to help him? "

"No Lord! I would have jumped in the water so fast to save him; he wouldn't have to say <u>anything</u>."

The Lord said, *"You're my child and you were drowning. I rescued you and spoke the words you needed to hear not because of what you said to me; it was because I love you".*

> Peace I leave with you, my peace I give unto you: not as the world giveth, give I unto you. Let not your heart be troubled, neither let it be afraid. John 14:27 KJV

GOOD INTENTIONS

You would be surprised how many people seemed to know the reason for Craig's death. Some said we loved him too much. I knew that was a lie because when I was first saved, the Lord woke me up three nights in a row, asking me if He was number one in my life. (See chapter about 'God's Chain of Order'.)

Every ounce of love that I had for Craig, God had given to me. Some said maybe because Tommy wasn't saved or there was unrepentant sin in my life. If that is solely true there would be very few children left in the world.

I was told God didn't take your little boy; the devil did. That made me angry. I didn't want him having anything to do with my son. I know the scripture says Satan has come to rob, steal and kill, but God is in control and the devil had to get permission from Him. I realize they were trying to defend God but God needed no defending. On and on it went until one comment broke the camel's back.

One day while working in the office a Christian lady came in. She was once a member of our church but left and started going to another church. I was glad to see her. She began to ask about Craig's accident and how I was doing. She said, *"I need to share something with you. If you would have known the **truth** Craig wouldn't have died. God doesn't want people to die".*

I said, *"How can you say that? He allowed His own son to die. You think we're more special than His own Son?"*

With that she left. It burnt me up...but then caused me to start questioning the things of God that I had been taught and believed.

I closed the office down and left to pick Brad up from school. This was the second time I heard that statement and I was starting to get confused. I was furious to think that I hadn't known or been taught the truth they kept talking about. I cried out, *"God please tell me...**WHAT IS THE TRUTH?**"*

He said, "***You know the truth...you know***

Jesus...Jesus is truth".

Through all the confusion and questions, I believe even though Craig's life was short he had completed his mission for the Lord. He was quite a preacher, singer and worshiper. Those who came in contact with him knew he loved the Lord. He was a God given gift to us and I can never thank the Lord enough for blessing us for three and a half years.

Jesus saith unto him, I am the way, the truth, and the life: no man cometh unto the Father, but by me.
John 14:6 KJV

TOMMY'S CHRISTIAN MOTHER

When I got saved in 1975, I called Mrs. Jones (Tommy's Mom), to tell her about the experience I had when I cried out to God at the stop light. I knew she was a true Christian and I trusted her to teach me what she knew. I remember asking God on Sundays to please help me stay saved until I could go back to church on Wednesday. At church on Wednesday, I would ask him to help me stay saved until Sunday.

I really didn't understand completely what had happened to me or what born again meant. That went on for a long time because I didn't want to lose what had happened to me. I had never had that kind of joy and peace in my life.

She told me she knew that I was born again for sure and not to worry because the Holy Spirit would keep and guide me into all truth. We talked on the phone every week. I don't know who was the happiest, me or her. She was so happy that her heathen daughter-in-law had finally gotten saved. Now she knew God would be working on her baby son.

Remembering:

CRAIG'S LAST EASTER SUNDAY

One morning, Craig turned on the TV that was on a Christian station, talking about the Holy Spirit. I don't know how that popped up because I didn't know anything about Christian TV. As I began to watch, and listen, my curiosity got the best of me. I called everybody I knew and their brothers and sisters to ask them what was the Holy Spirit about. No one could give me an answer except to say well, there's God the Father, His son Jesus and the Holy Spirit. They didn't know anything about Him.

I called a Pastor I knew who said it would take him 6 months to explain it to me. I wanted to know everything I could about the Lord and the Bible and I wanted to know now.

I began to watch Pastors Marvin Gorman and Jimmy Swaggarts' services on TV to see if I could find an answer about the Holy Spirit. I absolutely loved both of their programs.

As some of you know, Pastor Swaggart always says: "*Hallelujah, Hallelujah, Hallelujah*" or "*Praise the Lord, Praise the Lord, Praise the Lord*". He always says one or the other after singing a song. Well don't you know, Craig did the same thing, because he believed that's what you're supposed to do. That tickled me and Tommy because he was so serious.

When Craig was about 2 ½ yrs. old we went to spend Easter with Tommy's parents in Mississippi. We attended a Baptist church that Sunday morning with Mrs. Jones. She had Craig on her lap as we began to sing out of the hymn book. When the song was over, as customary with Craig, he hollered out: "*Hallelujah! Hallelujah! Hallelujah!*"

She tried to shush him but to no avail. After finishing the next song, she tried to shush him again but he hollered out: "*Praise the Lord! Praise the Lord! Praise the Lord!*".

The congregation giggled. I whispered to her that he wasn't going to stop until he said it 3 times like Jimmy

Swaggart. After church, some of them told me how cute he was, and how he sure wasn't embarrassed to praise the Lord out loud. That was just him because he truly loved the Lord.

I will bless the LORD at all times: His praise shall continually be in my mouth. Psalm 34:1 KJV

Remembering:

JESUS LOVES ME

One Sunday night getting ready to go to church, I told my youngest son Craig, he couldn't go because it was too cold and rainy and he had been having a runny nose. He began to cry and beg me to let him go but I kept telling him no.

Tommy saw what was going on and said: *"Why do you want to go to church?"*

He said, *"Because I love Jesus".*

Tommy said, *"Well why do you love Jesus?"*

Craig said, *"Because Jesus loves me".*

Tommy said, *"How do you know that?"*

He said, *"Because the bible tells me so".*

End of conversation (ha-ha). Needless to say, neither

one of us had the heart to argue anymore. He won the battle and I took him to church. Once at church he held onto the end of the pew singing and twisting his little biscuit hinny. I wouldn't take anything for that memory. Praise the Lord! Praise the Lord! Praise the Lord!

But Jesus said: Suffer little children, and forbid them not, to come unto me: for of such is the kingdom of heaven. Matt 19:14 KJV

TOMMY'S TESTIMONY

I was born and raised in Mississippi until I was 18 years old. I was also in the church up until that time. That's when I moved to Kenner LA. In fact, my family had already been there a year. I came down to work the summer before I graduated and I bought a car. My dad still owned his home in Mississippi. After the summer I went back home and lived by myself and graduated from the same school that I attended for 12 years.

I moved to Memphis TN and worked there a while but that didn't work out. So, I went back to Kenner, to live with my parents. That's when I met, Dottie, my future wife. We dated for 4 years and then married. It was almost 7 years before we had our first son Brad. He was a miracle and great blessing to us.

Then as life went on, during the next 2 to 3 years, we started having trouble with our marriage. It was almost over. We finally agreed to go to a counselor together. This helped a great deal and we worked things out. We just didn't have the right communication skills. She was one to argue and I wouldn't say anything.

Let me give some advice to young men reading this: arguing is a waste of time. Talk to each other and try to work things out. That will help you have a much better marriage.

Later on, Dottie got saved and I'm talking <u>saved</u> brother! She almost drove me crazy. I used to tell her if you're going to serve the Lord, you're going to have to go all the way. Well, that's what she did. Her life changed completely. I knew it was real. I had grown hard in my heart. I would not yield to God but she just kept loving me and Brad. We decided to have another child and had another son we named him Craig. Now we have two fine boys.

Tommy, Craig and Brad

We started getting the urge to move across the lake, north of Lake Pontchartrain. Our goal was to find waterfront property and we found what we were looking for in Lacombe LA. We built a nice home on side of Powell Bayou. Everything seemed to be going great.

We had been living there a year or so when I got up one Saturday morning to travel across the lake to work. I came back home that afternoon a little early. When I pulled up to the house, there were a few cars there. I had an uneasy feeling and felt like something was wrong. Before I could get out of my truck good, a couple of my neighbors met me and said: *"Come on inside there's something we have to tell you".*

I knew something was wrong when I walked in and saw Dottie. She was sitting in the chair and started crying when she saw me. I asked her: "*What's wrong? Where's the kids?*"

She said, "*Craig drowned a little while ago".*

I couldn't believe it. I kept asking, *"Are they sure he's not alive?"* I said, "*Let's go the hospital, I've got to see him"*.

Dottie said, "*He's not at the hospital, he's at the funeral home"*.

Well that just knocked everything right out of me. I just collapsed on the couch, sitting and staring into space. I didn't know how to handle this. It just so happened that Dottie had been looking for a church, and had attended Northlake Assembly of God, twice.

Before I got home that evening, a friend had called Pastor Cheshier from the church. (He was already at my house before I got there.) He came over to the couch where I was sitting and asked me and Dottie to go into the back bedroom so he could talk to us and pray. About that time his wife Marigold arrived and came into the room to join us.

They began ministering and praying for us. I asked Marigold, "*Why did God take my little son?'*

She said, "*I don't know, but just as King David's son couldn't come back from heaven, neither could Craig*".

She said, "*Tommy, you can't bring Craig back to you, but you can go to him*".

Well, that's when I gave my life to Christ, right then and there. God started giving me strength and hope, from that moment, until this very day. God worked everything out from where to bury him, how to bury him, the service, the preacher and even the finances.

We were at the funeral home making arrangements with my dad when he said: "*Son, you and Dottie pick out whatever you want. I'll pay for it*".

That was an answer to me from God, because I didn't know how I was going to handle it. I had never seen my dad carry that much cash. He pulled his wallet out and paid the funeral home in full. I tell you that did something to me.

At the wake that night I was touched by all the people who were there. Let me tell you something I learned. Don't worry about what you are going to say to the grieving family, just show up. That says more than any words can say.

At the funeral, there was a couple sitting there that we didn't know. Pastor Cheshier introduced them to us as Brother and Sister Norman Taylor from Northlake Assembly of God in Covington. They brought a ham and food from several other people in the congregation. Well that just touched my heart again.

My heart was so soft from just being born again that all these things happening were giving Dottie and I the strength we needed to bare this sorrow. These kinds of things just kept happening. We continued to get cards and letters of encouragement.

One man that we didn't even know sent us a card because he saw the death notice in the paper. He wrote some encouraging words and sent a large sum of cash. He said, "I've been there and I know where you are".

Come to find out he was the Santa Claus at the Lacombe Fire Station Christmas party that December. We had a picture of Craig sitting on his lap. When we found out who he was, we were able to personally thank him for reaching out to us.

A few months after Craig's death, I walked into a Time Saver one evening on my way home from work. There was a young man and his little boy in front of me. He reminded me of Craig. I said, "*God why did you take my son?*"

He answered right back and said: "*I never took your son, I chose him*".

That really ministered to me and I never asked that question again.

I was sitting at my dining room table one day just looking out the window at these little yellow butterflies.

They reminded me of Craig when he rode his tricycle around the yard just singing without a care in the world. The Lord spoke to my heart again, he said: *"You see that butterfly? Think of what he was before he became a butterfly. This is just a small example of Craig when he was on earth and his transformation now that he is with me".*

This was all happening during the time I was being healed by the Lord. I was in church now faithfully and reading God's Word. I just couldn't seem to get enough. The people of our church did just what they should have, they walked with us and are still walking with us today. I thank God for that church and I don't know what we would have done without them.

We continued to serve the Lord, and started having a Bible Study in our home, one night a week. Pastor Cheshier would come preach and teach. It grew so much that we had to move several times into larger buildings. Today there is a Living Word Assembly of God Church in Lacombe Louisiana that originated from the bible study.

And we know that all things work together for good to them that love God, to them who are the called according to His purpose. Romans 8:28 KJV

Someone sent us a poem called: Life's Weaving. It really encouraged us a lot and we send copies to others who are grieving to help encourage them. (See next page.)

Life's Weaving

My life is but a weaving Between my God and me; I may not choose the colors He knows what they should be; For He can view the pattern upon the upper side, While I can see it only, on this, the underside.

Sometimes He weaves sorrow, which seems strange to me; But I will trust His judgement, and work on faithfully; 'Tis He who fills the shuttle, He knows just what is best. So, I shall weave in earnest, and leave with Him the rest.

At last, when life is ended, with Him I shall abide. Then I may view the pattern, upon the upper side; Then I shall know the reason, why pain with joy entwined, was woven in the fabric, of life that God designed.

PHOTOS

Brad and Craig

Craig helping to clean the fridge

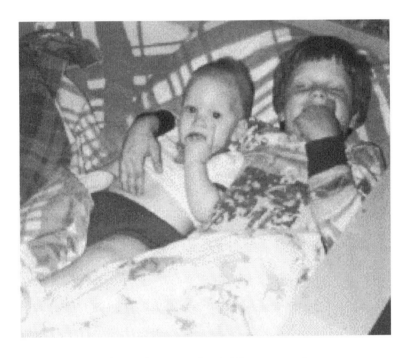

Craig and Brad in car bed. Two peas in a pod.

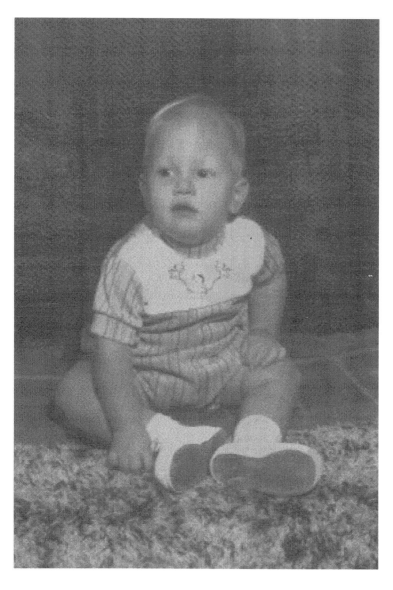

Craig at 1 Year Old

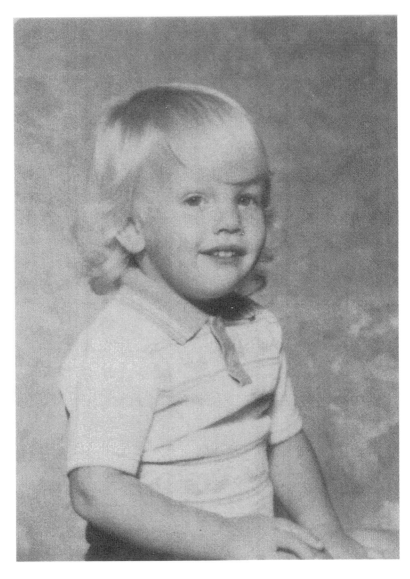

Craig at 2 Years Old

A Shattered Heart Restored!

To Order a copy, go to Amazon.com

Search by title and author name.

Made in United States
Orlando, FL
30 June 2022

19312682R00078